lonely planet

POCKET

SYDNEY

TOP EXPERIENCES · LOCAL LIFE

T0018190

ANDY SYMINGTON

Contents

Plan Your Trip

General Post Office (GPO; p61)
LEONID ANDRONOV/SHUTTERSTOCK ©

COVID-19

We have re-checked every business in this book before publication to ensure that it is still open after the COVID-19 outbreak. However, the economic and social impacts of COVID-19 will continue to be felt long after the outbreak has been contained, and many businesses, services and events referenced in this guide may experience ongoing restrictions. Some may be temporarily closed, have changed their opening hours and services, or require bookings; some unfortunately could have closed permanently. We suggest you check with venues before visiting for the latest information.

Top Experiences

Gaze at the Sydney Opera House

Visionary harbourside architectural masterpiece. **p32**

Walk Across the Sydney Harbour Bridge
Harbour crossing and Sydney icon. **p36**

Explore the Royal Botanic Garden
Verdant city-centre haven. **p34**

Discover Amazing Art at the Art Gallery of NSW
Treasury of Australian art, including stellar Indigenous artworks **p56**

Eat your Fill in Chinatown
Fascinating blend of cultures. **p58**

Learn About Aboriginal History at the Australian Museum Grande dame of Sydney museums. **p112**

Ride the Waves at Bondi Beach
Surf a legendary world beach. **p144**

Bike Around North Head
Fabulous walking; supreme harbour vistas. **p162**

Dining Out

Sydney's cuisine rivals that of any great world city. It truly celebrates Australia's place on the Pacific Rim, marrying the freshest local ingredients – excellent seafood is a particular highlight – with the flavours of Asia, the Mediterranean, the Americas and its colonial past. Sydneysiders are real foodies, always seeking out the latest hot restaurant.

Where to Eat

Sydney's top restaurants are properly pricey, but eating out needn't be expensive. There are plenty of budget places where you can grab a cheap, zingy pizza or a bowl of noodles. Cafes are a good bet for a solid, often adventurous and usually reasonably priced meal. Pubs either do reliable standard fare, often with excellent prices, or casual but high-quality Modern Australian dining. The numerous BYO (bring your own alcohol) restaurants offer a substantially cheaper eating experience; the inner west is brimful of them.

Vegetarians & Vegans

Sydney is great for herbivores. Unless you wander into a steakhouse by mistake, vegetarians should have no trouble finding satisfying choices on most menus. Some leading restaurants offer separate vegetarian menus, often stretching to multiple-course degustation.

The more socially progressive suburbs such as Newtown and Glebe have the widest range of veggie options. Surry Hills, Darlinghurst and Kings Cross also have good choices.

Best Restaurants

Quay Inventive fine dining with the best views in Sydney. (p42)

LuMi Inventive Italo-Japanese degustation in a quiet wharfside location in Pyrmont. (p82)

Mr Wong Hip Cantonese joint with perpetual queues out the door. (p68)

Ester Informal but innovative Modern-Australian dining. (p99)

Porteño Delicious slow-cooked meat and bucketloads of atmosphere. (p120)

TIMOTHY CHRISTIANTO/SHUTTERSTOCK ©

Tetsuya's A degustatory journey through multiple inventive courses. (p70)

Best Snacks & Sweets

Cow & the Moon Sydney's best ice-cream. (p93)

Bourke Street Bakery Irresistible pastries, cakes and bread. (p117)

Koi Dessert Bar Unbelievable dessert creations. (p96)

Best Cafes

Single O Still pioneering coffee. (p121)

Grounds of Alexandria Amazing organic farm-cafe. (p95)

Reuben Hills Brunches with a Latin American twist. (p118)

Trio Fight for a seat at this Bondi star. (p153)

Pablo & Rusty's The city centre's best coffee. (p67)

Wedge Narrow but quality-packed Glebe cafe. (p94)

Best Vegetarian & Vegan

Yellow Upmarket vegetarian degustation menus are memorably good. (p138)

Golden Lotus Crisp and fresh Vietnamese vegan fare in Newtown. (p94)

Lentil As Anything Heartening pay-what-you-want social project. (p94)

Funky Pies Who took the meat out of an Aussie icon? (p152)

Best Seafood

Boathouse on Blackwattle Bay Lovely Glebe location overlooking the water. (p100)

Flying Fish At the end of a Pyrmont pier, and boasting super views. (p84)

Golden Century Meet your meal in the tanks on the way in. (p71)

Azuma Sushi and sashimi of stratospheric quality. (p69)

Bar Open

In a city where rum was once the main currency, it's little wonder that drinking plays a big part in the Sydney social scene – whether it's knocking back some tinnies at the beach, schmoozing after work or warming up for a night on the town. Sydney offers plenty of choice in drinking establishments, from the flashy to the trashy.

The Sydney Scene

The relaxation of licensing laws has seen a blooming of 'small bars' in the city centre and inner suburbs. These are great spots, often difficult to find and with a quirky atmosphere, though the drinks don't come cheap.

The local pub, traditionally called a hotel because the liquor laws once meant they had to offer accommodation to serve booze, survives throughout the city. Often on corners, these venerable gems have been improved in recent years by beer gardens, upgraded food menus and a stupendous array of local craft beers.

Door Policies

Sydney's bouncers are often strict, arbitrary and immune to logic. Being questioned and searched every time you want a drink after 8pm on a weekend can definitely take the edge off a Sydney night out.

It is against the law to serve people who are intoxicated and you won't be admitted to a venue if you appear drunk. Expect to be questioned about how much you've had to drink that night.

Be prepared to present photo ID with proof of your age.

Lockouts

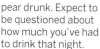

In an effort to cut down on alcohol-fuelled violence, tough licensing laws have been introduced to a large area of the central city. Within this zone, licensed venues are not permitted to admit people after 1.30am. However, if you arrive before then, the venue is permitted to continue serving

COOLR/SHUTTERSTOCK ©

you alcohol until 3am, or 3.30am in the case of certain venues which you can enter until 2am.

Best Historic Pubs

Hero of Waterloo Sturdy stone stalwart in the Rocks (p45)

Lord Nelson One of three claiming the title of 'oldest pub'. (p46)

Fortune of War Beautiful front bar. (p47)

Courthouse Hotel A slice of an older Newtown. (p102)

Shakespeare Hotel Gloriously traditional Sydney boozer in Surry Hills. (p124)

Best Outdoor Drinking

Watsons Bay Beach Club Take a ferry to this summer and weekend classic. (p159)

Opera Bar Is there a better-located bar in the world? (p45; pictured)

Glenmore Roof deck with great Opera House views. (p46)

Beresford Hotel Mixed crowd and quality wine and food. (p124)

Best Small Bars

Baxter Inn Whisky-laden city speakeasy. (p71)

Grandma's Kitsch retro basement hideaway. (p73)

Uncle Ming's Low-lit den of dumplings and cocktails. (p71)

Barber Shop Get a short back and sides on your way in. (p72)

Best Dancefloors

Frankie's Pizza Pizza slices, live bands, a nightclub...who needs more? (p71)

Ivy Glam inner-city location with Sydney's top club night. (p71)

Lazybones Lounge Gloriously louche and welcoming Inner West nightspot. (p100)

Arq Flashy and upmarket club in LGBTIQ+ heartland. (p126)

Treasure Hunt

Shopping is the number-one recreational activity for many in consumerist Sydney. Retail covers a wide range here, from glitzy city-centre boutiques to tourist shops, to Paddington galleries and grungy Newtown vintage stores. Best of all are the markets, with a really buzzy weekend scene – an essential Sydney experience.

Shopping Areas

Sydney's city centre is brimming over with department, chain and international fashion stores and arcades – shopping here is about as fast and furious as Australia gets. Paddington is the place for art and fashion, while new and secondhand boutiques around Newtown and Surry Hills cater to a hipper, more alternative crowd. Double Bay, Mosman and Balmain are a bit more 'mother of the bride', and if you're chasing bargains, head to Chinatown or the Alexandria factory outlets.

Newtown and Glebe have lots of book and record shops, though the city centre has good options too. For surf gear, head to Bondi or Manly. Woollahra, Newtown (around St Peters station) and Surry Hills are good for antiques. For souvenirs – from exquisite opals to tacky T-shirts – try the Rocks, Circular Quay and Darling Harbour.

What to Buy

Want something quintessentially Australian to take home? Head to the Rocks and dig up some opals, an Akubra hat, a Driza-Bone coat or some Blundstone boots. Aboriginal art makes an excellent purchase, but make sure it is ethically sourced.

Sydney has a thriving fashion scene, and a summer dress or Speedos won't eat up luggage space. Ask at music stores or bookshops about local bands and authors. Hunter Valley wine makes a great gift – check your country's duty-free allowance before buying.

KOKKAI NG/GETTY IMAGES ©

Taxes and Refunds

Sales taxes are included in the advertised price. Apart from the 10% goods and services tax (GST), the only other sales duties are on things such as alcohol and tobacco, which are best bought at duty-free shops, such as those at the airport. The GST tourist refund scheme (p183) has mostly replaced traditional duty-free shopping.

Best Markets

Paddington Markets Sydney's most famous market, selling everything from clothing to palm-reading. (p109; pictured)

Bondi Markets Fruit and veg on Saturdays, assorted bric-a-brac on Sundays. (p157)

Glebe Markets One big counter-cultural get-together. (p107)

Carriageworks Farmers Market Foodies flock here on Saturday mornings. (p105)

Best Jewellery

Paspaley Pearls from north-west Australia. (p75)

Opal Minded Get the classic Aussie gemstone. (p49)

Best Aboriginal Art

Gannon House Gallery Inspiring selection in the Rocks. (p49)

Artery Great range, from original works to printed souvenirs. (p127)

Karlangu Wide selection near Wynyard station. (p75)

Best Bookshops

Gleebooks Well-loved Glebe bookshop, with regular author talks. (p107)

Abbey's Brilliant inner-city bookshop, especially good on history, languages and sci-fi. (p74)

Better Read Than Dead Well-presented and -stocked Newtown store (p107)

Show Time

Take Sydney at face value and it's tempting to unfairly stereotype its good citizens as shallow and a little narcissistic. But take a closer look: the arts scene is thriving, sophisticated and progressive. Spectator sports, led by rugby league, are huge and attending a match is highly recommended.

Classical Music & Opera

There's a passionate audience for classical music in Sydney. Without having the extensive repertoires of European cities, Sydney offers plenty of inspired classical performances – the perfect excuse to check out the interior of the famous harbourside sails of the Sydney Opera House (p32). The City Recital Hall (p73) is another venue, with excellent acoustics.

Australia has produced some of the world's most ear-catching opera singers, including Dames Nellie Melba and Joan Sutherland.

Live Bands

Since the 1950s Sydney has been hip to jazz, and in the 1970s and '80s, Aussie pub rock became a force to be reckoned with. Sydney's live-music scene took a hell of a hit in the 1990s, when lucrative poker machines were first allowed in pubs, and hasn't really recovered. That said, you can catch bands any night of the week in various pubs, espe-

cially around the Inner West. Check the free street mags (*The Music* is the best; www. themusic.com.au) and Friday's *Sydney Morning Herald* for listings.

Spectator Sports

Australia's national self-esteem is so thoroughly intertwined with sporting success that locals worship their teams as they would a religion. Sport dominates weekend TV schedules, but nothing beats catching a game live.

GIRLWANDER1982/SHUTTERSTOCK ©

Rugby league is Sydney's all-consuming passion: a superfast, supermacho game with a frenzied atmosphere for spectators.

In rugby union and cricket, whipping the Kiwis, Poms and South Africans into submission is the name of the game, while in the national Australian Football League (AFL) and soccer competitions, Sydney's teams hold their own.

Women's sport has traditionally been underfunded and underwatched, but has an increasingly high profile as sports-mad Sydney gradually wakes up to it.

Best Entertainment Venues

Sydney Opera House Don't miss a chance to see the House in action. (p48)

State Theatre We don't care what's on – visiting this beautiful place is a joy. (p74; pictured)

City Recital Hall The city's premier classical-music venue. (p73)

Belvoir St Theatre Consistently excellent productions in an intimate setting. (p127)

Best Places for Live Bands

Oxford Art Factory Live indie bands, DJs and assorted bohemian happenings. (p127)

Lansdowne Hotel Bands upstairs most nights. (p105)

Camelot Lounge Two separate stages with interesting programming. (p104)

Metro Theatre Excellent sightlines and acoustics for midsize touring rock acts. (p73)

Beaches

The beach is an essential part of the Sydney experience. Its ocean beaches broadly divide into the eastern beaches, which are south of the harbour, running from Bondi southwards, and the northern beaches, north of the harbour, starting at Manly. The numerous harbour beaches are mostly east of the bridge on both the north and south sides.

AI_YOSHI/GETTY IMAGES ©

Need to Know

Always swim between the red-and-yellow flags on lifesaver-patrolled beaches.

If you get into trouble, hold up your hand to signal to the lifesavers.

Due to pollution from stormwater drains, avoid swimming in the ocean for a day and in the harbour for three days after heavy rains.

Ocean Pools

Sydney is blessed with a string of 40 man-made ocean pools up and down the coast, most of them free. Some, like Mahon Pool (p151; pictured), are what are known as bogey holes – natural-looking rock pools where you can safely splash about and snorkel, even while the surf surges in. Others are more like swimming pools; Bondi's Icebergs (p145) is a good example of this kind. They normally close one day a week so they can clean the seaweed out.

Best Beaches

Bondi Beach Australia's most iconic ocean beach. (p144)

Nielsen Park The pick of the harbour beaches, surrounded by beautiful national park. (p159)

Bronte Beach Family-friendly and backed by a park, this is an Eastern Suburbs gem. (p150)

Whale Beach Peachy-coloured sand and crashing waves; you've really left the city behind at this stunning Northern Beaches haven. (p173)

For Kids

Sydney offers something for everyone when it comes to kids' activities. Outdoorsy children will love the city's surf schools, bike tours or rope courses. On rainy days, kids can sate their curiosity at the Powerhouse Museum or the Art Gallery of NSW. Younger children will adore the brilliant dinosaur exhibition at the Australian Museum.

SAKARET/SHUTTERSTOCK ©

Active Pursuits

Kids can get lessons at surf schools, tackle the rope courses at Sydney Olympic Park and Taronga Zoo or go on a bike tour.

Sydney Harbour Kayaks (☏02-9960 4389; www.sydneyharbourkayaks.com.au; Smiths Boat Shed, 81 Parriwi Rd, Mosman; kayaks/SUP per hour from $20/25, ecotours $125; ⊙9am-5pm Mon-Fri, from 7.30am Sat & Sun, closed Mon & Tue Jun-Sep; 🚌E66, E68, E71, E75, 76, 77). Over-12s are welcome to tours, if they're with an adult. Families with over-threes can rent kayaks.

Indoor Options

Kids adore Ultimo's science-focused Powerhouse Museum. Australian Museum is a real hit with children especially its excellent dinosaur exhibition. You'll be surprised by the child-friendly Art Gallery of NSW; there are also regular art safaris and creative workshops at the MCA. Little astronomers might want to do some stargazing at the Sydney Observatory.

Babysitting

Most big hotels offer babysitting services. Otherwise, agencies can send babysitters to you, usually for a four-hour minimum (per hour from $25) and a booking fee (from $23)

Best For Kids

Royal Botanic Garden, along with most of Sydney's beaches & parks (p34; pictured)

Sydney Sea Life Aquarium (p81)

Australian National Maritime Museum (p79)

Powerhouse Museum (p92)

Taronga Zoo (p51)

Australian Museum (p112)

Luna Park (p51)

Sydney Observatory (p40)

LGBTIQ+

CATHERINE SUTHERLAND/LONELY PLANET ©

Sydney's LGBTIQ+ community is visible, vibrant and an integral part of the city's social fabric. Partly because central Sydney is so well integrated, and partly because of smartphone apps facilitating contact, the gay nightlife scene has died off substantially. But the action's still going on and Sydney is indisputably one of the world's great queer cities.

Mardi Gras

The Sydney Gay & Lesbian Mardi Gras (p176) is now Australia's biggest tourist date. While many focus on the parade, the LGBTIQ+ community throws itself into the entire festival, including the wild partying that surrounds it. Both are held on the first Saturday in March.

Social Acceptance

Acceptance of the LGBTIQ+ community has been a long, but successful fight.

The 2017 survey on gay marriage, which resulted in its legalisation, nevertheless revealed a split between conservative and liberal areas of Sydney on the issue.

LGBTIQ+ Venues

Arq The city's hottest gay dancefloor. (p126)

Imperial Hotel The legendary home of Priscilla, Queen of the Desert. (p103)

Palms on Oxford Goodtime, trashy, camp dance venue.

Stonewall Hotel Several levels of shiny, happy people. (p126)

LGBTIQ+ Shopping

Bookshop Darlinghurst Longstanding gay bookshop and a great source of local information. (p129)

Sax Fetish Racks of shiny black leather and rubber gear. (p128)

Gertrude & Alice Named after literary lesbians and packed with interesting reads. (p157)

Sappho Books, Cafe & Wine Bar Part bohemian cafe-bar, part rag-tag bookshop. (p89)

Lesbian Hangouts

McIver's Baths Coogee's legendary women-only sea baths. (p151)

Under the Radar

A lot of visitors to Sydney focus on the city centre, missing some fantastic experiences beyond it. For a vibrant dining scene, try Summer Hill, Crows Nest or the Vietnamese restaurants of Cabramatta. For colonial history, head to Parramatta. Surf beach? Hit Avalon or Cronulla. Cool bars and pubs? Get the train to Redfern or Marrickville.

RICHARDMILNES/SHUTTERSTOCK ©

Walk Away

The Bondi-to-Coogee and Spit Bridge to Manly walks are popular, but busy. Thankfully, it's easy to find just-as-spectacular walking elsewhere. Try heading south from Coogee to Maroubra, getting a ferry to Cremorne Point and walking to Balmoral Beach. For spectacular bushwalking in native forests, get to **Lane Cove** (weekdays 02-8448 0400, weekends 02-9472 8949; www.nationalparks. nsw.gov.au; Lady Game Dr, Chatswood West; per car

$8; ⊙9am-6pm Apr-Sep, to 7pm Oct-Mar; ☐545, 550, ☒North Ryde; pictured) or **Ku-ring-gai Chase National Park** (☏02-9472 8949; www. nationalparks.nsw.gov.au; per car per day $12, landing fee by boat adult/child $3/2; ⊙sunrise-sunset) in the city's north .

Museums and Galleries

Justice & Police Museum Hidden in plain sight right by Circular Quay. (p41)

Artspace Cutting-edge art and design right across from glitzy Woolloomooloo Wharf. (p135)

Chau Chak Wing Museum Head to beautiful Sydney University for this excellent multi-faceted museum. (p89)

White Rabbit A fabulous gallery of Chinese contemporary art. (p92)

Underrated Historic Buildings

Vaucluse House William Wentworth's Vaucluse mansion is a rare surviving colonial estate. (p159)

Elizabeth Bay House A harbourside home built in a gracious Georgian style. (p135)

Elizabeth Farm Sydney's oldest colonial house is part of this early farmhouse. (p53)

Four Perfect Days

Day One

THORSTEN RUST/SHUTTERSTOCK ©

Start at Circular Quay and head directly to **Sydney Opera House** (p32). Circle around it and then continue around the shoreline into the **Royal Botanic Garden** (p34). Have a good look around and then continue around **Mrs Macquaries Point** (p35) and along to the **Art Gallery of NSW** (p56), taking a detour into Woolloomooloo if you fancy some lunch. Take some time to explore the gallery then cross the **Domain** and cut through **Sydney Hospital** to Macquarie St. **Parliament House** (p61) is immediately to the right, while to the left is **The Mint** and **Hyde Park Barracks** (pictured; p64). Cross into **Hyde Park** (p61) and head straight through its centre, crossing Park St and continuing on to the **Anzac Memorial** (p66).

Day Two

MATTEO COLOMBO/GETTY IMAGES ©

Grab your swimming gear and head to the beach. Catch the bus to **Bondi Beach** (pictured; p144) and spend some time strolling about and soaking it all in. If the weather's right, stop for a swim in the sea or at **Icebergs Pool** (p145). Once you're done, take the **clifftop path** (p150) to **Tamarama** (p150) and on to **Bronte** (p150), both lovely bits of sand. Continue on the coastal path through **Waverley Cemetery** (p150) and down to **Clovelly** (p150). This is a great spot to stop for a swim or a snorkel. Continuing on you'll pass **Gordons Bay** and **Dolphin Point** before you arrive at **Coogee Beach** (p150), where you'll find lots of places to swim and some good spots for a beer afterwards.

Day Three

STEVE LOVEGROVE/SHUTTERSTOCK ©

Take a ferry from Circular Quay to **Watsons Bay** (p158). Watch the waves pound the cliffs at **The Gap** (p159), then continue on to **Camp Cove** (p159) for a dip. Take the **South Head Heritage Trail** (p159) for sublime views of the city and the harbour. After lunch, head back to Circular Quay and explore the Rocks. Start at the **Museum of Contemporary Art** (p40) and then head up into the network of lanes to the **Rocks Discovery Museum** (p40). Go through the Argyle Cut to **Millers Point** and up **Observatory Hill**. Pop into one of Sydney's oldest pubs – try the **Lord Nelson** (p46) or the **Hero of Waterloo** (pictured; p45) – then explore the wharves of **Walsh Bay** (p41), and double back under **Sydney Harbour Bridge** (p36).

Day Four

MAGSPACE/SHUTTERSTOCK ©

Have a stroll around the Darling Harbour waterfront and settle on whichever of the big attractions takes your fancy – perhaps the **Australian National Maritime Museum** (p79). Each of these will easily fill an entire morning. Next, jump on the river service at King St Wharf and take an hour-long cruise upstream as far as **Sydney Olympic Park**. Take a stroll around **Newington Nature Reserve** until the next ferry arrives to whisk you back. Stop at **Cockatoo Island** (pictured; p53) for a look at its art installations and the remnants of its convict and shipbuilding past. From here you can head back to Darling Harbour or Circular Quay.

Need to Know

For detailed information, see Survival Guide (p174)

Currency
Australian dollar ($)

Language Spoken
English

Visas
All visitors to Australia need a visa. New Zealand nationals receive a visa on arrival.

Money
ATMs are everywhere and major credit cards are widely accepted.

Mobile Phones
Local SIM cards are cheap. Using mobiles while driving is prohibited unless hands-free.

Time
Eastern Standard Time (GMT/UTC plus 10 hours)

Plugs & Adaptors
Standard voltage is 220 to 240 volts AC (50Hz). Plugs are flat three-pin types.

Tipping
If restaurant service is good, it is customary to tip (up to 10%).

Daily Budget

Budget: Less than $190
Dorm beds: $30–50
Return train trip: $8
Hanging out at the beach: free
Pizza, pasta, noodles or burgers: $10–20

Midrange: $190–320
Private room with own bathroom: $150–250
Cafe breakfast: $20–25
All-day public transport: maximum $15.40 using Opal card
Two-course dinner with glass of wine: $50–70

Top End: More than $320
Four-star hotel: from $250
Three-course dinner in top restaurant with wine: $140–250
Opera ticket: $160–350
Taxis: $50

Useful Websites

Destination NSW (www.sydney.com) Official visitors guide.

TripView The handiest app for planning public transport journeys.

Time Out (www.timeout.com/sydney) 'What's on' information and reviews.

Not Quite Nigella (www.notquite nigella.com) Entertaining food blog.

FBI Radio (https://fbiradio.com) Underground music and arts scene coverage.

Lonely Planet (www.lonelyplanet.com/sydney) Destination information, hotel bookings, traveller forum and more.

Arriving in Sydney

Most people arrive in Sydney by air, though you can arrive by bus and train from other Australian cities.

✈ Sydney Airport

10km south of city centre.

Taxis to the city cost up to $55 and depart from the front of the terminals

Airport shuttles head to city hotels for around $20

Trains depart from beneath the terminal but charge a whopping $13.80 on top of the normal train fare for the short journey into the city

🚇 Central Station

Country and interstate **trains** arrive at Central station, at the southern end of the city centre. Follow the signs downstairs to connect to local services or head to Railway Sq for buses.

🚇 Sydney Coach Terminal

Long-distance **coaches** stop in front of Central station.

⚓ Overseas Passenger Terminal

Many **cruise ships** pull in here, right on Circular Quay. There's a train station nearby.

Getting Around

Transport NSW (📞131 500; www.transportnsw.info) coordinates all of the state-run bus, ferry, train and light-rail services. The system-wide Opal transport card is necessary for travel. The TripView app is very useful for real-time public transport info and journey planning.

🚇 Train

The linchpin of the network, with lines radiating out from Central station.

🚌 Buses

Particularly useful for getting to the beaches and parts of the Inner West

⚓ Ferries

Head all around the harbour and up the river to Parramatta.

🚃 Light Rail (Tram)

Handy for Pyrmont, Glebe, Surry Hills, Moore Park, Randwick and city-hopping.

Ⓜ Metro

Under construction. The metro currently links northwestern Sydney with Chatswood; by the mid 2020s, it will go through the city centre and out to the west.

Advance Planning

Three months before Book accommodation; make sure your passport, visa and travel insurance are in order.
One month before Book top restaurants; check to see if your visit coincides with any major cultural or sporting events and book tickets.
A week before Top up your credit cards; check the Sydney news sites and 'what's on' lists.

Sydney Neighbourhoods

City Centre & Haymarket (p55)
Sydney's central business district offers plenty of choices for shopping, eating and sightseeing, with colonial buildings scattered among the skyscrapers.

Darling Harbour & Pyrmont (p77)
Unashamedly tourist focused, Darling Harbour tempts visitors to its shoreline bars and restaurants with fireworks displays and a sprinkling of glitz.

Inner West (p87)
Quietly bohemian Glebe and more loudly bohemian Newtown are the best known of the Inner West's tightly packed suburbs, which begin at the University of Sydney.

Sydney Harbour Bridge

Sydney Opera House

Royal Botanic Garden

Art Gallery of NSW

Chinatown

Australian Museum

Surry Hills & Darlinghurst (p111)
Home to a mishmash of inner-city hipsters, yuppies, a large LGBTIQ+ community, and an array of excellent bars and eateries.

North Head

Manly (p161)
The only place in Sydney where you can catch a ferry to swim in the ocean, Manly caps off the harbour with scrappy charm.

Circular Quay & the Rocks (p31)
The historic heart of Sydney, containing its most famous sights.

Kings Cross & Potts Point (p131)
Strip joints, tacky tourist shops and backpacker hostels bang heads with classy restaurants, boozy bars and gorgeous guesthouses.

Bondi to Coogee (p143)
Improbably goodlooking arcs of sand framed by jagged cliffs, the eastern beaches are a big part of the Sydney experience.

Bondi Beach

Explore
Sydney

Worth a Trip 🔭

Sydney's Walking Tours 🥾

Sky Safari cable car (p51) CONSTANTIN STANCIU/SHUTTERSTOCK ©

Explore

Circular Quay & the Rocks

The birthplace of the city, this compact area seamlessly combines the historic with the exuberantly modern. Join the tourist pilgrimage to the Opera House and Harbour Bridge, then grab a schooner at a convict-era pub in the Rocks.

Sydney Cove carries the twin stars of the city's iconography, with the Harbour Bridge (p36) and the Opera House (p32) abutting each end of its horseshoe. Circular Quay's promenade serves as a backdrop for buskers of mixed merit and locals disgorging from harbour ferries. The Rocks is unrecognisable from the squalid place it once was and now serves as an 'olde-worlde' tourist focus. Over the ridge is Millers Point, a low-key colonial district that makes a calming diversion from the harbourside tourist fray, and Walsh Bay, a handsome redeveloped maritime precinct.

Getting There & Around

🚇 Circular Quay is one of the City Circle train stations; Wynyard is also close by.

⛴ Circular Quay is Sydney's ferry hub, providing services all around the harbour.

🚌 Circular Quay is a terminus for several eastern suburbs bus routes.

🚊 Light rail travels from Circular Quay along George St to Central station and beyond.

Circular Quay & the Rocks Map on p38

The Rocks district at dusk M. LETSCHERT/SHUTTERSTOCK ©

Top Experience 📷
Gaze at the Sydney Opera House

Gazing upon the Sydney Opera House with virgin eyes is a sure way to send a tingle down your spine. Gloriously curvaceous and pointy, this landmark perches dramatically at the tip of Bennelong Point, waiting for its close-up. No matter from which angle you point a lens at it, it shamelessly mugs for the camera; it really doesn't have a bad side.

◎ MAP P38, G3

☎ 02-9250 7111

www.sydneyopera
house.com

Bennelong Point

tours adult/child $37/20

🕙 tours 9am-5pm

🚇 Circular Quay

Design & Construction

Danish architect Jørn Utzon's competition-winning 1956 design is Australia's most recognisable visual image. It's said to have been inspired by billowing sails, orange segments, palm fronds and Mayan temples, and has been likened to nuns in a rugby scrum, a typewriter stuffed with scallop shells and the sexual congress of turtles. It's not until you get close that you realise the seemingly solid expanse of white is actually composed of tiles – 1,056,000 self-cleaning cream-coloured Swedish tiles, to be exact.

Interior

Inside, dance, concerts, opera and theatre are staged in the **Concert Hall**, **Joan Sutherland Theatre**, **Drama Theatre** and **Playhouse**, while more intimate and left-of-centre shows inhabit the **Studio**. The acoustics in the concert hall are superb; the internal aesthetics like the belly of a whale.

Most events (2400 of them annually!) sell out quickly, but partial-view tickets are often available on short notice. The free monthly *What's On* brochure, available at tourist information points and at the Opera House itself, lists upcoming events, including info on the excellent children's programming – a pint-sized entertainment roster of music, drama and dance.

Tours

One-hour guided tours of the interior (adult/child $37/20) depart throughout the day. Not all tours can visit all theatres because of rehearsals, but you're more likely to see everything if you go early. A highlight is the **Utzon Room**, the only part of the Opera House to have an interior designed by the great man himself. For a more in-depth nose around, the two-hour, early-morning backstage tour ($169, departs 7am) includes the Green Room, stars' dressing rooms, stage and orchestra pit.

★ Top Tips

○ At the time of research, renovation works were due to take place until late 2021 or early 2022. Performance schedules and guided tours may be disrupted, so it's worth checking ahead to see how your visit may be affected.

✗ Take a Break

One of Sydney's finest restaurants, Aria (p43), is just opposite the Opera House; perfect for a gourmet pre- or post-show meal.

Opera Bar (p45), on the concourse below the Opera House, is a fabulous spot for a drink or a meal by the water.

Top Experience 📷

Explore the Royal Botanic Garden

This expansive park is the inner city's favourite picnic destination, jogging route and snuggling spot. Following the shore of Farm Cove, the bay immediately southeast of the Opera House, the garden was established in 1816 and features plant life from Australia and around the world. It also includes the site of the colony's first paltry vegetable patch.

◎ MAP P38, H5

📞 02-9231 8111

www.rbgsyd.nsw.gov.au

Mrs Macquarie's Rd

admission free

🕐 7am-dusk

🚉 Circular Quay

Collections

Highlights include the rose garden, the rainforest walk, and the succulent garden. The striking Calyx pavilion incorporates a cool, curving glasshouse space with a living wall of greenery that requires some 18,000 plants to fill. It hosts temporary exhibitions on botanical themes.

Government House

Surrounded by English-style grounds, **Government House** (☎02-9228 4111; www.governor.nsw. gov.au; Macquarie St; admission free; ⏰grounds 10am-4pm, tours 10.30am-3pm Fri-Sun) is a Gothic sandstone mansion (built 1837–43), which serves as the official residence of the Governor of NSW. Its lovely loggia looks over a formal garden with the Opera House looming close by.

Mrs Macquaries Point

Mrs Macquaries Point forms the northeastern tip of Farm Cove and provides beautiful views over the bay to the Opera House and city skyline. It was named in 1810 after Elizabeth, Governor Macquarie's wife, who ordered a seat chiselled into the rock from which she could view the harbour. **Mrs Macquaries Chair**, as it's known, remains to this day.

Walks and Tours

Free guided walks depart daily from the information booth outside the Garden Shop. You can also download self-guided tours from the RBG website. The park's paths are mostly wheelchair accessible.

Long before the convicts arrived, this was an initiation ground for the Gadigal (Cadigal) people. Book ahead for the **Aboriginal Heritage Tour** (☎02-9231 8134; www.rbgsyd.nsw.gov.au; adult $40; ⏰10am Wed, Fri & Sat), which covers local history, traditional plant uses and bush-food tastings.

★ **Top Tips**

o Estimated walking times on signs are pessimistic. If a sign says something is five minutes away, bank on two.

o If you're all walked out, take a ride on the **Choochoo Express** (www.choochoo.com. au; adult/child $10/5; ⏰11am-4pm May-Sep, 10am-4.30pm Oct-Apr), a trackless train that departs from Queen Elizabeth II Gate (nearest the Opera House) every half-hour.

✗ **Take a Break**

In the park itself, the **Botanic Gardens Restaurant** (☎02-9241 2419; www.botanic restaurant.com.au; lunch mains $29-34; ⏰noon-3pm Mon-Fri, from 9.30am Sat & Sun) offers quality food in a foresty environment.

End your stroll at the wharf at Woolloomooloo, where China Doll (p139) is an excellent venue for waterside dining.

Top Experience 📸

Walk Across the Sydney Harbour Bridge

Whether they're driving over it, climbing up it, jogging across it, shooting fireworks off it or sailing under it, Sydneysiders adore their bridge and swarm around it like ants on ice cream. Dubbed the 'coathanger', the harbour bridge is a spookily big object – moving around town, you'll catch sight of it out of the corner of your eye when you least expect it.

◎ MAP P38, E1

🚉 Circular Quay, Milsons Point

Structure

At 134m high, 1149m long, 49m wide and weighing 52,800 tonnes, Sydney Harbour Bridge is the largest and heaviest (but not the longest) steel arch in the world. It links the Rocks with North Sydney, crossing the harbour at one of its narrowest points. The two halves of chief engineer JJC Bradfield's mighty arch were built outwards from each shore. In 1930, after seven years of toil by 1400 workers, the two arches were only centimetres apart when 100km/h winds set them swaying. The coathanger hung tough, though; the arch was bolted together and the bridge finally opened to the public two years later.

BridgeClimb

Once only painters and daredevils scaled the Harbour Bridge – now anyone with a moderate level of fitness can do it. Make your way through the **BridgeClimb** (☎02-8274 7777; www.bridge climb.com; 3 Cumberland St; adult $258-383, child $178-273) departure lounge and the extensive training session, don your headset, an umbilical safety cord and a dandy grey jumpsuit and up you go. Tours last 2¼ to 3½ hours – a pre-climb toilet stop is a smart idea. The priciest climbs are at dawn and sunset. A cheaper, 90-minute 'sampler' climb (heading to a lower point) is also available, as is an 'express climb', which ascends to the top via a faster route.

Pylon Lookout Museum

The bridge's hefty pylons may look as though they're shouldering all the weight, but they're largely decorative – right down to their granite facing. There are awesome views from **Pylon Lookout** (☎02-9240 1100; www.pylonlookout.com. au; adult/child $15/8.50; ⊙10am-5pm), atop the southeast pylon. Inside the pylon there are exhibits about the bridge's construction, including an eight-minute film that screens every 15 minutes.

★ Top Tips

o The best way to experience the bridge is on foot – don't expect much of a view crossing by train or car (driving south there's a toll).

o Staircases access the bridge from both shores; a footpath runs along its eastern side and a cycleway along the west.

o The northern end of the bridge walk is very close to Milsons Point train station. Walking north to south offers the best views.

✗ Take a Break

The southern end of the bridge sits right among some of the best pubs in the Rocks. Try the rooftop at the Glenmore (p46) for more great views.

If it's a cafe you're after, make your way down to the Fine Food Store (p42), tucked away on a side street.

Circular Quay & the Rocks Walk Across the Sydney Harbour Bridge

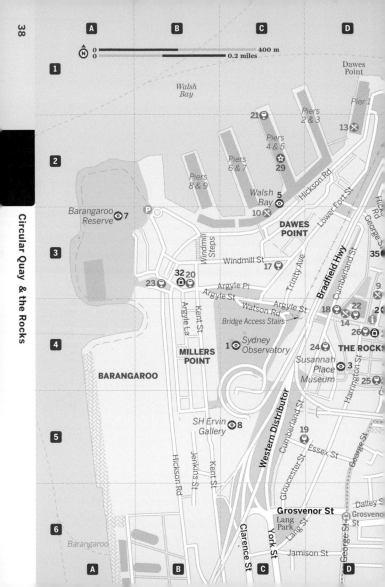

N

0
0

400 m
0.2 miles

Walsh
Bay

Dawes
Point

Pier 1

Piers
2 & 3

13

21

Piers
4 & 5

Piers
6 & 7

29

Piers
8 & 9

Walsh
Bay

5

Hickson Rd

10

DAWES
POINT

Barangaroo
Reserve

7

P

Lower Fort St

George St

35

Windmill Steps

Windmill St

17

Trinity Ave

Bradfield Hwy

Cumberland St

32 20

23

Argyle Pl

Argyle St

Watson Rd

Argyle St

18

22

9

14

26

2

Argyle La

Kent St

Bridge Access Stairs

1

Sydney
Observatory

24

THE ROCKS

MILLERS
POINT

Susannah
Place
Museum

3

Harrington St

25

BARANGAROO

SH Ervin
Gallery

8

Hickson Rd

Jenkins St

Kent St

Western Distributor

Cumberland St

19

Essex St

George St

Grosvenor St

Grosvenor
St

Clarence St

York St

Gloucester St

Lang Park

Lang St

Jamison St

George St

Dalley S

Barangaroo

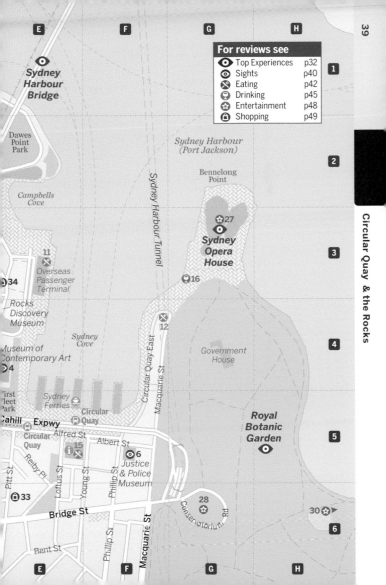

E **F** **G** **H**

For reviews see
👁	Top Experiences	p32
⊙	Sights	p40
✗	Eating	p42
🍷	Drinking	p45
✪	Entertainment	p48
🛍	Shopping	p49

Sydney Harbour Bridge

Dawes Point Park

Campbells Cove

Sydney Harbour (Port Jackson)

Bennelong Point

Sydney Harbour Tunnel

✪27
Sydney Opera House

🚉16

11
✗ Overseas Passenger Terminal

🛍34

Rocks Discovery Museum

Sydney Cove

✗12
Circular Quay East

Museum of Contemporary Art
🛍4

Government House

Sydney Ferries

Circular Quay

Macquarie St

Royal Botanic Garden
👁

First Fleet Park

Cahill Expwy

Circular Quay
ⓘ✗15

Alfred St

Albert St

⊙6
Justice & Police Museum

Retby Pl

Pitt St

Loftus St

Young St

Phillip St

🛍33

Bridge St

28
✪

Conservatorium Rd

30✪►

Bent St

Phillip St

Macquarie St

Sights

Sydney Observatory
OBSERVATORY

1 ⊙ MAP P38, C4

Built in the 1850s, Sydney's copper-domed, Italianate sandstone observatory squats atop **Observatory Hill**, overlooking the harbour. Inside is a collection of vintage apparatus, including Australia's oldest working telescope (1874), as well as background on Australian astronomy and transits of Venus. Also on offer (weekends and school holidays) are child-focused tours (adult/child $10/8), including a solar telescope viewing and planetarium show. Bookings are essential for night-time stargazing sessions, which come in family-oriented (adult/child $22/17) and adult (adult/child $27/20) versions. (📞02-9217 0111; www.maas.museum/sydney-observatory; 1003 Upper Fort St; admission free; ⊗10am-5pm; 🚉Circular Quay)

Rocks Discovery Museum
MUSEUM

2 ⊙ MAP P38, D4

Divided into four displays – Warrane (pre-1788), Colony (1788–1820), Port (1820–1900) and Transformations (1900 to the present) – this small, excellent museum, tucked away down a Rocks laneway, digs deep into the area's history on an artefact-rich tour. Sensitive attention is given to the Rocks' original inhabitants,

the Gadigal (Cadigal) people, and there are interesting tales of early colonial characters. (📞02-9240 8680; www.therocks.com; Kendall Lane; admission free; ⊗10am-5pm; 👣; 🚉Circular Quay)

Susannah Place Museum
MUSEUM

3 ⊙ MAP P38, D4

Dating from 1844, this diminutive terrace of four houses and a shop selling historical wares is a fascinating time capsule of life in the Rocks. After watching a short film about the past inhabitants, you will be guided through the claustrophobic homes, decorated to reflect different eras. The visit lasts an hour. Groups are limited to eight, so book ahead. (📞bookings 02-9251 5988; www.sydneyliving museums.com.au; 58-64 Gloucester St; adult/child $12/8; ⊗tours 2pm, 3pm & 4pm; 🚉Circular Quay)

Museum of Contemporary Art
GALLERY

4 ⊙ MAP P38, E4

The MCA is a showcase for Australian and international contemporary art, with a rotating permanent collection and temporary exhibitions. Aboriginal art features prominently. The art-deco building has had a modern space grafted on to it, the highlight of which is the rooftop cafe with stunning views. There are free guided tours every day, with several languages available. (MCA; 📞02-9245 2400;

Sydney Observatory

www.mca.com.au; 140 George St; admission free; ◎9am-5pm Wed, from 10am Thu-Tue; ◙Circular Quay)

Walsh Bay
WATERFRONT

5 ◉ MAP P38, C2

This section of Dawes Point waterfront was Sydney's busiest before the advent of container shipping and the construction of port facilities at Botany Bay. This century has seen the Federation-era wharves gentrified beyond belief, morphing into luxury hotels, apartments, theatre spaces, power-boat marinas and restaurants. It's a picturesque place to stroll, combining the wharves and harbour views with Barangaroo Park. (www. walshbaysydney.com.au; Hickson Rd; ◙324, 325, ◙Wynyard)

Justice & Police Museum
MUSEUM

6 ◉ MAP P38, F5

In a sandstone building that once headquartered the Water Police, this atmospheric museum plunges you straight into Sydney noir. An assemblage of black-and-white photos from police archives provide the backdrop for stories of gangs, murders, bushranging and underworld figures, as well as being a fascinating window into social history. The highlight is the magnificently laconic commentary on the audiovisual features. (☎02-9252 1144; www.sydneyliving museums.com.au; cnr Albert & Phillip Sts; adult/child $12/8; ◎10am-5pm Sat & Sun; ◙Circular Quay)

Barangaroo Reserve PARK

7 ⊙ MAP P38, A3

Part of Barangaroo, the major redevelopment project of what was a commercial port, this park sits on a headland with wonderful harbour perspectives. The tiered space combines quarried sandstone blocks and native trees and plants to good effect. A lift connecting the park's three levels is good for weary legs. There's a car park under it, and an exhibition space. (www.barangaroo.com; Hickson Rd; 🚌 324, 325, 🚈 Circular Quay)

SH Ervin Gallery GALLERY

8 ⊙ MAP P38, C5

High on the hill inside the old Fort St School (1856), the SH Ervin Gallery, though surrounded by freeway, is a pleasing oasis that exhibits invariably rewarding historical and contemporary Australian art. Annual mainstays include the Salon des Refusés (alternative Archibald Prize entries) and the Portia Geach Memorial Award. There's a cafe here, too. (☏ 02-9258 0173; www.shervingallery.com. au; Watson Rd; adult/child $10/free; ⊙ 11am-5pm Tue-Sun; 🚈 Wynyard)

Eating

Fine Food Store CAFE $

9 ⊗ MAP P38, D3

The Rocks sometimes seems all pubs, so it's a delight to find this contemporary cafe that works for a sightseeing stopover or a better,

cheaper breakfast than your hotel. Staff are genuinely welcoming, make very respectable coffee and offer delicious panini, sandwiches and other breakfast and lunch fare. The outside tables on this narrow lane are the spot to be. (☏ 02-9252 1196; www.finefoodstore. com; cnr Mill & Kendall Lanes; light meals $9-16; ⊙ 7am-4pm Mon-Sat, from 7.30am Sun; 🛜 🖋; 🚈 Circular Quay)

Barcycle CAFE $

10 ⊗ MAP P38, C3

One of several inviting spots for a light meal on the handsome wharves of Walsh Bay, this hole-in-the-wall is run by a friendly Italian family who offer a range of breakfast and lunch options including 'green eggs' with avocado, pasta, salads and daily specials. The coffee is pretty good, as is the cycling chat: there's an on-site bike workshop here. (☏ 02-9247 0772; www.barcycle.com. au; Pier 6-7, 19 Hickson Rd; light meals $10-15; ⊙ 7am-4pm Mon-Sat, to 3pm Sun, later on Fri & Sat evenings in summer; 🛜; 🚌 324, 325, 🚈 Circular Quay)

Quay MODERN AUSTRALIAN $$$

11 ⊗ MAP P38, E3

What many consider to be Sydney's best restaurant matches a peerless bridge view with brilliant food. Chef Peter Gilmore never rests on his laurels, consistently delivering exquisitely crafted, adventurous cuisine – you can rely on amazing creations. Book online well in advance, but it's worth phoning in case of cancellations. (☎02-9251 5600; www.quay.com.au; Level 3, Overseas Passenger Terminal; 4/8 courses $180/245; ⏱6-9.30pm Mon-Thu, noon-1.30pm & 6-9.30pm Fri-Sun; 🚇Circular Quay)

Aria

MODERN AUSTRALIAN $$$

12 ✖ MAP P38, F4

Aria is a star in Sydney's fine-dining firmament, an award-winning combination of chef Matt Moran's stellar dishes, floor-to-ceiling windows staring straight

A Gritty Past

ⓘ

After dismissing Botany Bay as a site for the colony, Governor Phillip sailed the First Fleet into what James Cook had named Port Jackson (Warran/Warrane in the local language) and dropped anchor at a horseshoe bay with an all-important freshwater stream running into it. Phillip christened the bay Sydney Cove after the British Home Secretary, Baron Sydney of Chislehurst, who was responsible for the colonies.

The socioeconomic divide of the future city was foreshadowed when the convicts were allocated the rocky land to the west of the stream (known unimaginatively as the Rocks), while the governor and other officials pitched their tents to the east.

Built with convict labour between 1837 and 1844, Circular Quay was originally (and more accurately) called Semicircular Quay, and acted as the main port of Sydney. In the 1850s it was extended further, covering over the by-then festering Tank Stream, which ran into the middle of the cove. As time went on, whalers and sailors joined the ex-convicts at the Rocks – and inns and brothels sprang up to entertain them. With the settlement filthy and overcrowded, the nouveau riche started building houses on the upper slopes, their sewage flowing to the slums below. Residents sloshed through open sewers, and alleys festered with disease and drunken lawlessness. Thus began a long, steady decline.

Bubonic plague broke out in 1900, leading to the razing of entire streets, and Harbour Bridge construction in the 1920s wiped out even more. It wasn't until the 1970s that the Rocks' cultural and architectural heritage was finally recognised.

Much of Millers Point has been public housing for over a century, originally for dock workers. With property prices so high, the State government from 2016 began a series of phases of auctioning off these homes to the highest bidder, evicting one of Sydney's oldest communities in the process and ignoring significant public protest.

Bennelong

Bennelong was born around 1764 into the Wangal tribe, the westerly neighbours of the Gadigal (Cadigal) who lived around central Sydney. Captured in 1789, he was brought to Governor Arthur Phillip, who hoped to use Bennelong to understand the local Aboriginal Australians' customs and language.

Bennelong took to life with the settlers, developing a taste for British food and alcohol, and learning to speak the language of his new 'masters'. Eventually he escaped, but he returned by 1791 when reassured that he would not be held against his will. He developed a strong friendship with Governor Phillip, who had a brick hut built for him on what is now Bennelong Point.

The relationship between Phillip and Bennelong was a fascinating one, and included the governor being speared by an associate of Bennelong while visiting a beached sperm whale at Manly Cove. It may be that it was a kind of ritual payback; Phillip took no retaliation.

In 1792 Bennelong went on a 'civilising' trip to England, and returned in 1795 with a changed dress sense and altered behaviour. Described as good natured and 'stoutly made', Bennelong ultimately was no longer accepted by Aboriginal society and never really found happiness with his white friends either. He died a broken, dispossessed man in 1813.

at the Opera House, a stylishly renovated interior and faultless service. A pre- and post-theatre à la carte menu is perfect for a special meal before or after a night at the Opera House (one/two/three courses $55/90/110). (☏02-9240 2255; www.ariarestaurant.com; 1 Macquarie St; 2-/3-/4-course dinner $115/145/170, degustation $205; ⊗noon-2.15pm & 5.30-10.30pm Mon-Fri, noon-1.30pm & 5-11pm Sat, noon-1.45pm & 5.30-10pm Sun; ⓡCircular Quay)

Gantry
MODERN AUSTRALIAN $$$

13 ✪ MAP P38, D2

Despite all that water, there aren't too many harbourside restaurants in this area. Fortunately, Gantry is excellent. Try a wharfside table and enjoy views of Walsh Bay with a screen to protect you from sun and stickybeaks. The food, impeccably sourced from high-quality Australian producers, is delicious, with some standout fish usually on the menu and good vegetarian options. (☏02-8298 9910; www.thegantry.com.au; Wharf 1, 11 Hickson

Rd; mains $36-42; ⏰6-10pm Mon &
Tue, noon-2.30pm & 6-10pm Wed-Sun;
🛜🅿; 🚌324, 325, 🚉Circular Quay)

Saké
JAPANESE $$$

14 🍴 MAP P38, D4

Colourful sake barrels and lots of
dark wood contribute to the louche
glamour of this large, buzzy restau-
rant. Prop yourself around the open
kitchen and snack on delectable
popcorn shrimp and maki rolls, or
grab a table to tuck into multi-
course banquets of contemporary
Japanese cuisine. (🕿02-9259 5656;
www.sakerestaurant.com.au; 12 Argyle
St; mains $28-46; ⏰noon-3pm & 5.30-
10.30pm Mon-Thu, to 11.30pm Fri & Sat,
to 10pm Sun; 🚉Circular Quay)

Cafe Sydney
MODERN AUSTRALIAN $$$

15 🍴 MAP P38, E5

This breezy, spacious restaurant
on the roof of the **Customs House**
(🕿02-9242 8551; www.sydney
customshouse.com.au; admission free;
⏰8am-midnight Mon-Fri, from 10am
Sat, 11am-5pm Sun) has marvel-
lous harbour and bridge views, an
outdoor terrace, a glass ceiling, a
cocktail bar and friendly staff who
greet you straight out of the lift.
Quality seafood dishes dominate.
It packs out and is often block-
booked, so don't expect to show
up and get a table. (🕿02-9251
8683; www.cafesydney.com; Level 5,
Customs House, 31 Alfred St; mains
$37-40; ⏰noon-11pm Mon-Fri, from
5pm Sat, noon-3.30pm Sun; 🛜;
🚉Circular Quay)

Drinking

Opera Bar
BAR

16 🍺 MAP P38, G3

Right on the harbour with the
Opera House on one side and the
bridge on the other, this perfectly
positioned terrace manages a very
Sydney marriage of the laid-back
and the sophisticated. It's an
iconic spot for visitors and locals
alike. There's live music or DJs
most nights and really excellent
food, running from oysters to
fabulous steaks and fish.

It's a very slick operation...
staff even geolocate you to know
where to bring the food to. (🕿02-
9247 1666; www.operabar.com.au;
lower concourse, Sydney Opera House;
⏰10.30am-midnight Mon-Thu, to 1am
Fri, 9am-1am Sat, to midnight Sun; 🛜;
🚉Circular Quay)

Hero of Waterloo
PUB

17 🍺 MAP P38, C3

Enter this rough-hewn 1843
sandstone pub to meet some
locals, chat to the Irish bar staff
and grab an earful of the swing,
folk and Celtic bands (Friday to
Sunday). Downstairs is a dungeon
where, in days gone by, drinkers
would sleep off a heavy night
before being shanghaied to the
high seas via a tunnel leading to
the harbour. (🕿02-9252 4553; www.
heroofwaterloo.com.au; 81 Lower Fort
St; ⏰10am-11.30pm Mon-Wed, 10am-
midnight Thu-Sat, 10am-10pm Sun;
🚌311, 🚉Circular Quay)

Glenmore Hotel

PUB

18 📍 MAP P38, D4

Downstairs it's a predictably nice old Rocks pub with great outdoor seating, but head to the rooftop and the views are beyond fabulous: Opera House (after the cruise ship leaves), harbour and city skyline all present and accounted for. It gets rammed up here on the weekends, with DJs and plenty of wine by the glass. The food's decent too. (📞02-9247 4794; www.theglenmore.com.au; 96 Cumberland St; ⏰11am-midnight Sun-Thu, to 1am Fri & Sat; 📶; 🚊Circular Quay)

Harts Pub

PUB

19 📍 MAP P38, C5

Pouring an excellent range of Sydney craft beers in a quiet corner near the beginning of the Rocks, this historical building has real character. The dishes are quality pub food, with excellent and generous salads, fish and steaks. At weekends, this is enjoyably quieter than other Rocks boozers. There are a few pleasant outdoor tables with the **Shangri-La** (📞02-9250 6000; www.shangri-la. com; 176 Cumberland St; r $350-600; 🅿❄📶♨) looming above. (📞02-9251 6030; www.hartspub. com; cnr Essex & Gloucester Sts; ⏰noon-11pm Mon-Wed, 11.30am-midnight Thu, to 1am Fri & Sat, noon-10pm Sun; 📶; 🚊Circular Quay)

Lord Nelson Brewery Hotel

BREWERY

20 📍 MAP P38, B3

This atmospheric boozer is one of three claiming to be Sydney's oldest (all using slightly different criteria). The on-site brewery cooks up its own natural ales; a pint of dark, stouty Nelson's Blood is a fine way to partake. Pub food downstairs is tasty and solid; the upstairs brasserie is an attractive space doing fancier food, including good seafood choices. (📞02-9251 4044; www.lordnelsonbrewery.com; 19 Kent St; ⏰11am-11pm Mon-Sat, noon-10pm Sun; 📶; 🚌311, 🚊Circular Quay)

Theatre Bar at the End of the Wharf

BAR

21 📍 MAP P38, C2

It's a long but atmospheric stroll down this wharf building, looking at photos of Sydney Theatre Company performances as you go, to reach the bar at the end. It's a cracking spot, with a magic view of the Harbour Bridge to enjoy with a drink. Also does lunches from noon to 3pm (mains $18 to $28). (📞02-9250 1761; www.sydneytheatre. com.au; Pier 4, 15 Hickson Rd; ⏰noon-11pm Mon-Sat; 📶; 🚌324, 325, 🚊Circular Quay)

Argyle

BAR, CLUB

22 📍 MAP P38, D4

This stylish and wildly popular conglomeration of bars is spread through the historic Argyle Stores buildings, including a cobble-stone courtyard and atmospheric wooden-floored downstairs bar. The decor ranges from rococo couches to white extruded plastic tables, all offset with kooky chandeliers and moody lighting. During the day the courtyard is a pleasant place for a drink or spot of lunch. (☎02-9247 5500; www.theargylerocks.com; 18 Argyle St; ⏱11am-1am Sun-Wed, to 3am Thu-Sat; 🛜; 🚆Circular Quay)

Hotel Palisade   PUB

23 🔵 MAP P38, B3

This historic and hipster-invigorated Millers Point pub preserves its tea-coloured tiles, faded brick and nostalgia-tinted downstairs bar. On top of the venerable building, however, there's a shiny glass section with super bridge views, pricey drinks and posh tapas-style food. It often fills up or books out, but there's a less glitzy, more comfy perch on the little 4th-floor balcony. (☎02-9018 0123; www.hotelpalisade.com; 35 Bettington St; ⏱noon-midnight Mon-Sat, to 10pm Sun; 🛜; 🚌311, 🚆Circular Quay)

Australian Hotel   PUB

24 🔵 MAP P38, D4

With its wide verandah shading lots of outdoor seating, this handsome early 20th-century pub is a favoured pit-stop for a cleansing ale; it was doing microbrewed beer long before it became trendy and has a great selection. The kitchen

Fortune of War

CLAUDINE VAN MASSENHOVE/SHUTTERSTOCK ©

/GETTY IMAGES ©

also does a nice line in gourmet pizzas ($17 to $28), including ever-popular toppings of kangaroo, emu and crocodile. (☎02-9247 2229; www.australianheritagehotel.com; 100 Cumberland St; ⏱11am-midnight; 🛜; 🚆Circular Quay)

Fortune of War   PUB

25 🔵 MAP P38, D4

Operating right here since 1828, this pub was rebuilt in the early 20th century and retains much charm from that era in its characterful bar. It has a solid mix of locals and tourists, and features live music on Thursday, Friday and Saturday nights and weekend afternoons. (☎02-9247 2714; www.fortuneofwar.com.au; 137 George St; ⏱9am-midnight Mon-Wed, to 1am Thu, to 2am Fri & Sat, 10am-midnight Sun; 🚆Circular Quay)

Endeavour Tap Rooms

MICROBREWERY

26 ⏺ MAP P38, D4

All corridors and slightly awkward spaces, this heritage building in the heart of the Rocks is now a rather lovely brewpub with restrained 1920s-feel decor. There's some top stuff on tap, including the perfectly balanced Australian IPA and other excellent beers. A menu of meaty, smoky fare is on hand. (📞02-9241 6517; www.taprooms.com.au; 39 Argyle St; ⏲11am-midnight Mon-Sat, to 10pm Sun; 🛜; 🚉Circular Quay)

Entertainment

Sydney Opera House

PERFORMING ARTS

27 ⭐ MAP P38, G3

The glamorous jewel at the heart of Australian performance, Sydney's famous Opera House has five main stages. Opera has star billing, but it's also an important venue for theatre, dance and classical concerts, while big-name bands sometimes rock the forecourt. Renovation works through to early 2022 may disrupt some performances, but essentially the show goes on. (📞02-9250 7777; www.sydneyoperahouse. com; Bennelong Point; 🚉Circular Quay)

Sydney Conservatorium of Music

CLASSICAL MUSIC

28 ⭐ MAP P38, G6

This historic venue showcases the talents of its students and their teachers. Choral, jazz, operatic and chamber concerts happen from March to November; check the website (and Facebook page, which often has more info) for details. There are often free recitals. (📞02-9351 1222; http://music. sydney.edu.au; Conservatorium Rd; 🚉Circular Quay)

Sydney Theatre Company

THEATRE

29 ⭐ MAP P38, C2

Established in 1978, the STC is Sydney theatre's top dog and has played an important part in the careers of many famous Australian actors (especially Cate Blanchett, who was co-artistic director from 2008 to 2013). You can book tours of the company's **Wharf** and **Roslyn Packer Theatres** (📞02-9250 1999; www.roslynpackertheatre.com.au; 22 Hickson Rd; tours $10). Performances are also staged at the Opera House. (STC; 📞02-9250 1777; www.sydneytheatre. com.au; Pier 4, 15 Hickson Rd; ⏲box office 9am-7.30pm Mon, to 8.30pm Tue-Fri, 11am-8.30pm Sat, 2hr before show Sun; 🚌324, 325, 🚉Circular Quay)

OpenAir Cinema

CINEMA

30 ⭐ MAP P38, H6

Right on the harbour, the outdoor three-storey screen here comes with surround-sound, sunsets, skyline and swanky food and wine. Most tickets are purchased in advance – look out for the dates in early December as they go fast – but a limited number go on sale at the door each night at 6.30pm; check the website for details. (📞1300 366 649; www.stgeorgeopenair.com.au; Mrs Macquaries Rd; tickets $39; 🕐Jan & Feb; 🚊Circular Quay)

Shopping

Gannon House Gallery

ART

31 🔒 MAP P38, D4

Specialising in contemporary Australian and Aboriginal art, Gannon House purchases works directly from artists and Aboriginal communities.

You'll find the work of prominent artists such as Gloria Petyarre here, alongside lesser-known names. There are always some striking and wonderful pieces. (📞02-9251 4474; www.gannonhousegallery.com; 45 Argyle St; 🕐10am-6pm; 🚊Circular Quay)

Craft NSW

ARTS & CRAFTS

32 🔒 MAP P38, B3

This craft association gallery is full of beautiful and original creations. It's the perfect spot to pick up a unique gift for someone special. (📞02-9241 5825; www.artsandcraftsnsw.com.au; 12 Argyle Pl; 🕐10am-5pm)

Australian Wine Centre

WINE

33 🔒 MAP P38, E6

This store, with multilingual staff, is packed with quality Australian wine, beer and spirits. Smaller producers are well represented, as is a staggering range of prestigious Penfolds Grange wines and other bottle-aged gems. Service is excellent and international shipping can be arranged. (📞02-9247 2755; www.australianwinecentre.com; 42 Pitt St; 🕐10am-7pm Mon & Sun, 9.30am-8pm Tue & Wed, to 9pm Thu-Sat; 🚊Circular Quay)

Opal Minded

JEWELLERY

34 🔒 MAP P38, E3

This shop in the Rocks is one of several spots around here where you can stock up on opal, that quintessential piece of Aussie bling. The quality and service are both excellent. (📞02-9247 9885; www.opalminded.com; 55 George St; 🕐9am-6.30pm; 🚊Circular Quay)

The Rocks Markets

MARKET

35 🔒 MAP P38, D3

Under a long white canopy, the stalls at this market are a focus for tourists, but the excellent handicrafts outweigh the amount of koala tat. Pick up tasty treats at the 'Foodies Market' on Fridays or gifts at the weekends. (www.therocks.com/markets; George St; 🕐9am-3pm Fri, 10am-5pm Sat & Sun; 🚊Circular Quay)

Worth a Trip 🔭

Harbour Highlights

There's nothing better in Sydney than being out on the harbour, and using local ferry services to do your sightseeing is a great experience. You could visit most of these waterside spots in a busy day of ferry-hopping, but take a full day to see Taronga Zoo in the detail it deserves.

Trip Details

Ferries from Circular Quay, some government-run, some private, visit all these spots, some on a hop-on hop-off basis.

Taronga Zoo

A 12-minute ferry ride from Circular Quay, this bushy harbour hillside **zoo** (02-9969 2777; www.taronga. org.au; Bradleys Head Rd, Mosman; adult/child $46/26; 9.30am-5pm Sep-Apr, to 4.30pm May-Aug; ; 238, 247, M30, Taronga Zoo) is full of kangaroos, koalas and other hirsute Australian animals, plus numerous imported guests. The zoo's critters have million-dollar harbour views, but seem blissfully unaware of the privilege. Encouragingly, Taronga sets benchmarks in animal care and welfare. Highlights include the nocturnal platypus habitat, the Great Southern Oceans section and the Asian elephant display. Feedings happen throughout the day.

Catching the ferry is part of the fun. From the wharf, the **Sky Safari** cable car or a bus will whisk you to the entrance, from which you can traverse the zoo downhill back to the ferry.

Luna Park

A sinister clown face (pictured) forms the entrance to this old-fashioned **amusement park** (02-9922 6644; www.lunaparksydney.com; 1 Olympic Dr, Milsons Point; admission free; 11am-10pm Fri & Sat, 10am-6pm Sun, 11am-4pm Mon; Milsons Point, Milsons Point) overlooking Sydney Harbour. It's one of several 1930s features, including the Coney Island funhouse, a pretty carousel and the nausea-inducing Rotor. You can purchase a two-ride pass ($20), or buy a height-based unlimited-ride pass (adults $52, kids $22 to $42, cheaper online).

McMahons Point

Is there a better view of the Bridge and the Opera House than from the wharf at this **point** (Henry Lawson Ave; McMahons Point)? Only a short hop by ferry northwest of the city centre, the vista is all unfolded before you: it's a stunning spot to be when the sun is setting.

Garden Island

The majority of this naval base is off-limits, but you can visit the tip by ferry. There's a pleasant garden and lookout as well as a cafe and a **naval museum** (02-9359 2003; www.navy.gov.au; admission free; 9.30am-3.30pm; Garden Island). It's a modern display with wartime paraphernalia, weapons, submarine control consoles and a periscope you can use to observe the harbour.

Fort Denison

In colonial times this small **island** (restaurant 02-9361 5208, tour bookings 1300 72757; www.fortdenison.com. au; tour plus ferry adult/child $37.50/29; tours 11.15am, 12.15pm, 2pm & 3.10pm; Fort Denison) was used to isolate convicts and nicknamed 'Pinchgut' for its meagre rations. Fears of Russian invasion during the Crimean War led to its fortification. The **NPWS** (1300 072 757; www.nationalparks.nsw.gov.au) offers tours of the tower (prebook online), although many people just pop over for lunch at the outdoor restaurant.

Worth a Trip 👀

Upriver to Parramatta

Sydney Harbour gets all the attention, but a jaunt upriver is just as interesting. As you pass old industrial sites and the Olympic complex, or gaze into millionaires' backyards, a window opens onto a watery world in the heart of Sydney. Parramatta combines treasures from the earliest days of European colonization with ambitious modern development.

Trip Details

The F3 ferry line runs from Circular Quay to Parramatta (1¼ hours) via Cockatoo Island (also served by F8 ferries). It's faster but less scenic to reach Parramatta by train.

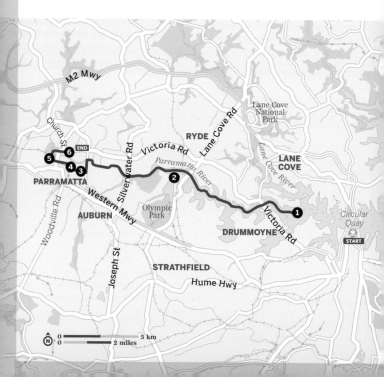

❶ Explore
Cockatoo Island

Ferry from Circular Quay to fascinating **Cockatoo Island** (🖉02-8969 2100; www.cockatooisland.gov.au; 🚢Cockatoo Island). Studded with industrial relics, convict architecture and art, it opened to the public in 2007. Information boards and audio guides ($5) explain the island's various uses as a prison, a shipyard and a naval base. A spooky tunnel passes clear through the middle.

❷ Up the River

Catch the F3 ferry from Cockatoo Island upriver towards Parramatta. You'll pass 640-hectare **Sydney Olympic Park** before disembarking at **Parramatta**, founded in 1788 by Governor Phillip, who needed a place to grow grain to supply the colony. Big things are afoot in Parramatta, which is undergoing a massive and ambitious development program.

❸ Elizabeth Farm

Walk east from the ferry stop to **Elizabeth Farm** (🖉02-9635 9488; www.sydneylivingmuseums.com.au; 70 Alice St, Rosehill; adult/child $12/8; ⏰10am-4pm Wed-Sun; 🚉Rosehill, 🚉Harris Park when Rosehill is closed), which contains part of Australia's oldest surviving colonial building (1793), built by pastoralist and rum trader John Macarthur. The homestead is now a hands-on museum where you can sit on the reproduction furniture and read Elizabeth Macarthur's letters.

❹ Experiment
Farm Cottage

Near Elizabeth Farm, this **colonial bungalow** (🖉02-9635 5655; www.nationaltrust.org.au; 9 Ruse St, Harris Park; adult/child $9/4; ⏰guided tours 10.30am-3.30pm Wed-Sun; 🚉Harris Park) stands on the site of Australia's first official land grant in 1789. The house, built around 1835, is decked out in period style with lovely early-colonial furniture. Entrance is by an informative guided tour.

❺ Old Government House

Walk through the rapidly-changing centre of Parramatta to Parramatta Park, a lovely riverside spot containing **Old Government House** (🖉02-9635 8149; www.nationaltrust.org.au; Parramatta Park, Parramatta; adult/child $14/6; ⏰10am-4pm Tue-Sun; 🚉Parramatta), the oldest remaining public building in Australia (1799). Temporary exhibitions add to the building's interest and there's a vine-draped courtyard restaurant.

❻ A Riverside Stroll

Cross the bridge across the river and head back east along the **bankside path**. It's a lovely stroll that will take you back to the ferry, where you can sip a drink at the adjacent bar/restaurant while you wait. If you want to get back to town more quickly, head for Parramatta train station instead.